A New True Book

ASTRONOMY

By Dennis B. Fradin

This "true book" was prepared
under the direction of
Illa Podendorf,
formerly with the Laboratory School,
University of Chicago

 CHILDRENS PRESS, CHICAGO

This large cloud of dust and gas found
in the Milky Way is called the Veil Nebula.

PHOTO CREDITS

Finley Holiday Film—6, 7, 8, 9 (2 photos), 10
(2 photos), 13 (2 photos), 18, 21, 26, 27
(2 photos), 28 (2 photos), 29 (2 photos),
31 (2 photos), 38

Historical Pictures Service, Chicago—15
(4 photos), 16, 41 (2 photos), 42

NASA: National Aeronautics and Space
Administration—32

Lynn M. Stone—23

John Forsberg—25, 35, 36

U.S. Naval Observatory—cover, 2, 4
(2 photos), 45 (2 photos)

COVER—Messier 20, in the Trifid Nebula

Library of Congress Cataloging in Publication Data

Fradin, Dennis B.
  Astronomy.

  (A New true book)
  Includes index.
  Summary: Presents basic information about the stars,
constellations, galaxies, universe, Earth, and solar
system and briefly discusses space travel and
astronomers.
    1. Astronomy—Juvenile literature. [1. Astronomy]
I. Title.
QB46.F76 1983   523   82-19722
ISBN 0-516-01673-3   AACR2

TABLE OF CONTENTS

Sagittarius star cloud

Close-up of the surface of the moon

LOOKING AT THE SKY

Have you ever looked at the sky on a clear night? It is beautiful. The stars sparkle. The moon looks close enough to touch. If you know where to look, you might even see a planet or two.

Stars and large cloud of dust and gas (Helix Nebula) found in the night sky

Those who have looked at the night sky have been introduced to astronomy. Astronomy is the study of the stars, planets, and other heavenly bodies.

THE STARS

Stars are balls of hot, glowing gas. With your eyes, you can see about 2,000 stars. With a telescope, you can see many millions of stars.

Cluster of stars

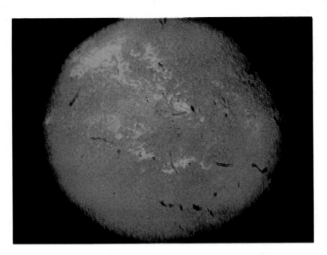

The sun photographed in
a special light
called hi-alpha light

The sun is a star. It looks big because it is so close to Earth. The sun is a yellow star.

Some stars are bluish white. Others are white, orange, yellow, or red. The colors of stars show how hot they are. Blue-white stars are the hottest. Red stars are the coolest.

Close-up of the Horsehead Nebula in Orion

Another large mass of dust and gas is named the Dumbbell Nebula.

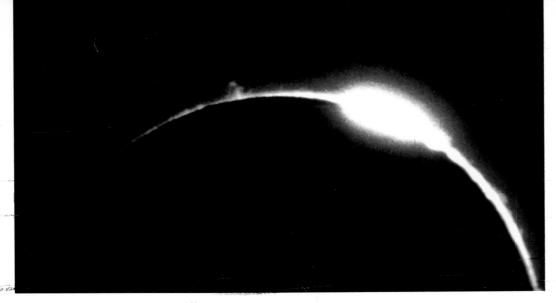

Diamond ring effect on the sun visible during a solar
eclipse. A solar eclipse happens when the moon passes
between the sun and the Earth.

The sun is a star. It gives the Earth heat and light.

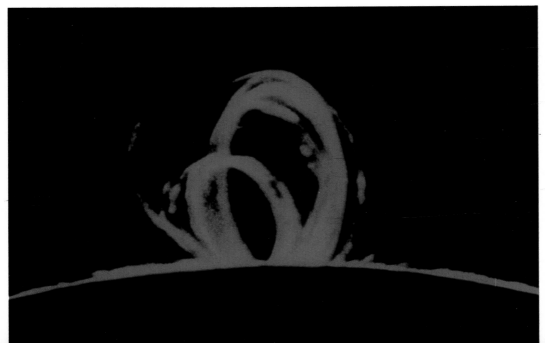

Stars come in all sizes. More than a million Earths could fit inside the sun. Yet the sun is just an average-sized star.

The biggest stars are called supergiants. The red supergiant Antares can be seen in the summer sky. It is one of the largest stars known. If Antares were located in the sun's place, it would extend all the way beyond our planet Earth.

The tiniest stars are called neutron stars. They are only a few miles across.

How far away are the stars? VERY FAR! The sun, which is the closest star to Earth, is 93 million miles away. Proxima Centauri, the closest star after the sun, is 25 trillion miles away. Other stars are still much farther away.

There are billions of stars in the universe. Skylab (below) sent back thousands of pictures of outer space.

CONSTELLATIONS

Have you ever played connect-the-dot? You draw lines between the dots to make a picture. Ancient people looked at stars and played connect-the-dot in their minds. "That group of stars looks like a hunter!" they said. "Those look like twin boys!"

The ancients gave names to the star groups.

The group that looked like a man with a club they named Orion, the Hunter. The group that looked like twin boys they called Gemini, the Twins.

The ancient astronomers gave names to the star groups, such as Pisces (below left), Gemini (below), Sagittarius (right), and Taurus (below right).

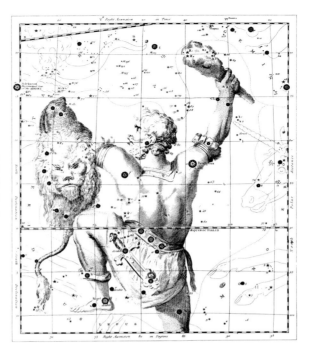

Orion, the Hunter. Astronomers used these ancient star pictures to divide their star maps into constellations.

They made up stories about the stars. For example, near Orion is a star group called Canis Major, the Big Dog. The ancients said that Canis Major was Orion's hunting dog. It could be seen that

Canis Major was a faithful dog. He always stayed near Orion in the sky!

Today we call these pretend star pictures constellations. Astronomers still find it useful to divide their star maps into constellations.

Go outside on a clear night. See if you can find some of the constellations.

A meteoroid (made up of particles of stone or metal) shoots through the night sky against the background of the Milky Way.

THE MILKY WAY AND OTHER GALAXIES

Have you ever seen a white patch stretching across the summer sky at night? That white patch is called the Milky Way.

The Milky Way is made up of billions of stars. The Milky Way has so many stars that it looks solid white. Through a telescope, the separate stars in the Milky Way can be seen.

The Milky Way is our galaxy—a very large group of stars moving together through space. The sun is part of the Milky Way galaxy. So are all the stars you can see with your eyes.

Using telescopes, astronomers have seen millions of other galaxies. Many look like patches of white light shaped like

A galaxy is a group of millions of stars. This one is a Spiral Galaxy.

pinwheels. Each galaxy has millions of stars, just like the Milky Way. From very far away, the Milky Way would look like a pinwheel-shaped patch of light, too.

THE UNIVERSE

Astronomers have a word to describe space and everything that is in it. They call it the universe. All the planets, stars, and galaxies are in the universe. Everything is in the universe.

How big is the universe? Astronomers don't know. Some think it may have no end.

Sunrise in a salt marsh

THE SOLAR SYSTEM

The sun is only an average star in the Milky Way galaxy. But the sun is special to life on Earth. Without it, none of us would be here.

Sun

Mercury

Venus

Moon

Earth

Mars

Jupiter

Many objects, including the planets, orbit the sun. The sun and all objects that orbit it are called the solar system.

The sun is the biggest member of the solar system. The sun is hot, eleven thousand degrees

at its surface. Inside, it is
many millions of degrees
hotter. The sun provides
heat and light for
everything in our solar
system.

Nine large objects orbit
the sun. They are the
planets.

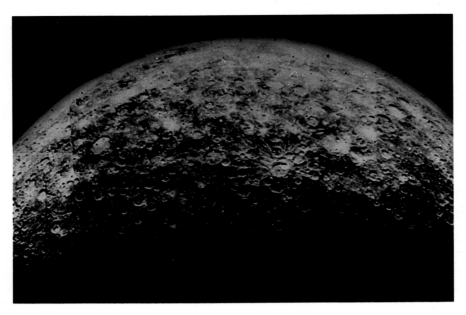

Mercury

Mercury is the closest planet to the sun. Its surface is hotter than a baker's oven.

Venus is the second planet from the sun. It can often be seen before dawn or just after sunset. Venus

Earth

Venus

looks bright white because of the thick clouds that cover it.

Mercury and Venus are too hot to support beings like ourselves. But the third planet from the sun is just right. You live on that planet now. It is Earth.

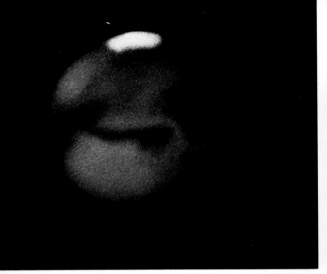
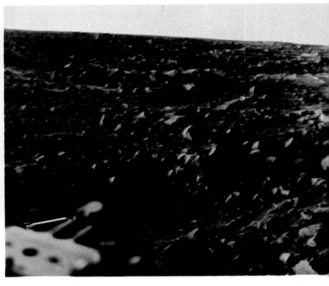

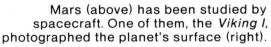

Mars (above) has been studied by spacecraft. One of them, the *Viking I*, photographed the planet's surface (right).

Mars, the red planet, is fourth from the sun. People once thought that animals or even people might live on Mars. But space probes have shown that Mars has little water and air. Mars does have one thing Earth doesn't. It has two moons instead of one.

Jupiter, fifth from the sun, is the largest planet. Pretty colored clouds cover Jupiter. Through a small telescope, four of Jupiter's sixteen moons can be seen.

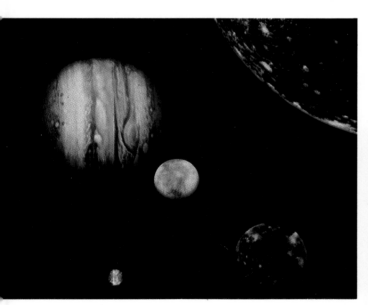

Left: A look at Jupiter and four of its sixteen moons
Below: Jupiter is covered by clouds.

Saturn, sixth from the sun, is one of the loveliest sights in the universe. Saturn has rings. Possibly they were formed when one of Saturn's moons exploded and began circling the planet.

Uranus, Neptune, and Pluto are the seventh, eighth, and ninth planets from the sun. The

Above: Saturn
Left: Close-up of the multi-colored rings
       around Saturn

temperature is 240
degrees below zero, or
colder, on all three.
Astronomers are still
looking for more planets
beyond Pluto.

The solar system has other objects besides the sun, the planets, and the moons. Now and then comets, including the

This comet, named Kohoutek, was photographed in 1974 streaking through our solar system.

famed Halley's Comet, appear in the sky. Comets are made of ice, gas, and dust. Between Mars and Jupiter there are rocky objects called asteroids. In addition, there are particles called meteoroids throughout the solar system. Meteoroids that burn up in Earth's air are called meteors.

OUR PLANET EARTH

You may not think of Earth as an object in space. But it is. There are many reminders of this fact.

Night and day are constant reminders. In the morning, the sun appears to rise. It seems to move across the sky and then set at night. But the sun isn't really moving across the sky. The sun appears

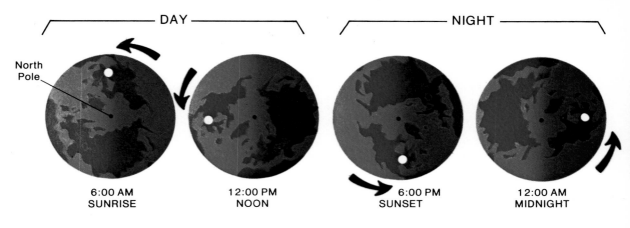

North Pole

SUN

6:00 AM
SUNRISE

12:00 PM
NOON

6:00 PM
SUNSET

12:00 AM
MIDNIGHT

Follow the white dot to see how the Earth spins

to rise and set because the Earth is spinning like a merry-go-round.

When our side of the planet is facing the sun, we have daylight. When our side of Earth spins away from the sun, we have night. The Earth takes 24 hours—one day—to spin once.

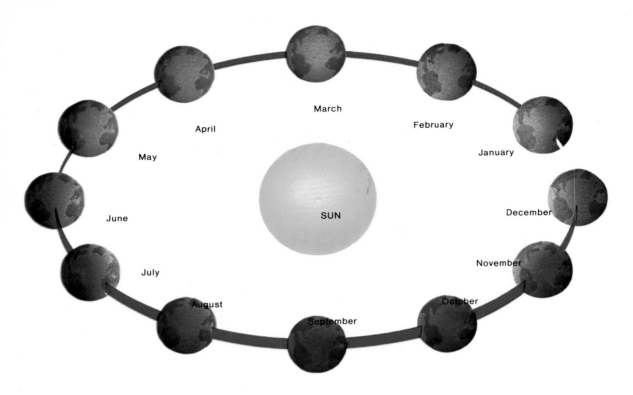

As the earth rotates, it also orbits the sun.

Earth does more than spin. It also moves in a big, egg-shaped orbit around the sun. It takes Earth 365 days—one year—to orbit the sun.

SPACE TRAVEL

People have always dreamed about exploring space. In this century we have done it.

In 1957 Russia sent up the first satellite to orbit Earth. It was called *Sputnik I*. On July 20, 1969, United States astronauts Neil Armstrong and Edwin Aldrin became the first people to walk on the moon. In the 1970s the United States launched spacecraft to study the planets. These spacecraft sent back photos of the planets and other data.

Rocket carrying the Skylab spacecraft lifts off.

It would be nice to find a world like our own out in space. But it appears that no planet in the solar system is anything like Earth. None has the right kind of air or enough water to support human beings. All are either too hot or too cold.

But there are many other stars besides the sun. Some of those stars might have planets like Earth.

ASTRONOMERS

Men and women who study the stars are called astronomers. Many famous astronomers have helped us understand the universe.

Long ago, people thought Earth was the center of everything. The Polish astronomer Nicolaus Copernicus said that Earth wasn't the center of things. He was right, but few people agreed with him.

Left: Nicolaus Copernicus
(NIK • oh • lus Koh • PER • nik • kuss)
(1473-1543)
Above: Galileo (gal • ih • LEE • oh)
(1564-1642)

When the Italian astronomer Galileo said that the Earth went around the sun, he was put in jail. Today we know that Copernicus and Galileo were right. They are remembered as great astronomers.

Sir Isaac Newton
(1642-1727)

The English scientist Sir Isaac Newton explained the force called gravity.
Earth's gravity holds us down to the ground. The sun's gravity holds the planets in position. It keeps them from flying off into space.

Using telescopes, astronomers have made many discoveries. The American astronomer Edwin Hubble studied galaxies. He discovered that the Milky Way is just one of many galaxies. He helped us realize that our Earth is one planet going around one sun in one galaxy.

THE FUTURE
OF ASTRONOMY

Astronomers are always making new discoveries. But many questions in astronomy remain unanswered. How did the solar system begin? How big is the universe? Do distant stars have planets with life on them?

Above: Dome of a telescope at
Flagstaff, Arizona
Left: Base of this telescope

Future astronomers will try to answer those questions. Perhaps you will become an astronomer. Then you may help to answer such questions yourself.

WORDS YOU SHOULD KNOW

asteroids(AST • er • oyds) — rocky objects located between Mars and Jupiter

astronauts(AST • roh • nauts) — space explorers

astronomer(ast • RON • ih • mer) — a person who studies stars, planets, and other heavenly bodies

Big Dipper(BIG DIP • er) — a well-known constellation

comets(COM • etz) — objects (made of ice, gases, and dust) that have long glowing tails when near the sun

constellation(kon • stel • AY • shun) — a star group in a certain area of the sky

galaxy(GAL • axee) — a group of millions of stars moving together through space

gravity(GRAV • ih • tee) — the force that holds us down to Earth

light year — the distance that light, which moves at 186,000 miles per second, travels in a year; astronomers use the light year to measure immense distances

meteoroids(MEAT • ee • or • oids) — particles of stone or metal in the solar system

meteors(MEAT • ee • ores) — meteoroids that appear as streaks of light when they burn up in Earth's atmosphere

Milky Way(MIL • kee WAY) — a galaxy with billions of stars, including the sun

million(MILL • yun) — a thousand thousand (1,000,000)

moon — a natural object that orbits a planet

nebula(NEB • yoo • la) — a very large cloud of dust and gas found in the Milky Way and in other galaxies

North Star — a star in the Little Dipper that is due north

orbit(OR • bit) — the path an object takes when it moves around another object

planet(PLAN • it) — an object that orbits a star

radio telescopes(RAY • dee • oh TEL • ih • skohpz) — instruments that collect radio waves from distant objects